DENNY
REMEMBERED

DENNY REMEMBERED

DENNIS WILSON IN WORDS AND PICTURES

Edward Wincentsen

Wynn Publishing

Wynn Publishing
P.O. Box 1491
Pickens, SC 29671

First Printing, January 1991
Second Printing, August 1999
(Revised Edition)

Library of Congress Card Number: 90-071134

ISBN: 0-9642808-3-3

The following song lyrics have been used by permission of the Publishers:

"FOREVER" by Dennis Wilson and Gregg Jakobson
© 1970 Brother Publishing and Daywin Music, Inc.
All Rights Reserved.

"THE D.W. SUITE" Written by Lindsey Buckingham
©1984 Now Sounds Music
All Rights Reserved.

"ONLY OVER YOU" written by Christine McVie
© 1982 Fleetwood Mac Music
All Rights Reserved.

Book Design: Ed Wincentsen

Typesetting: Dianna Burrup / Apple MacIntosh ®

Front Cover Photo: © 1979, 1990 Ed Roach

Dedicated
to
Rachel Summers
Who had a spirit
for life like Denny

and to

Denny's children:
Jennifer,
Michael,
Carl,
Gage,
and Scott
who love him
most of all.

Contents

The D. W. Suite
by Lindsey Buckingham

A. "The Wish"

If we go, go insane
We can all go together
In this wild, wanton
 world
We can all break down
 forever . . .

I want to go
Go forever
I want to go
Go forever
Its just a memory
Its just a memory . . .
Gone forever . .

B. "The Prayer"

The closing of a chapter
The opening of a door
Brings forth life
Where there was no
 life before
I won't be here, I'll be
 watching from above
Always do what you should
Always be good
When push comes to shove
Pray for guidance from
 above

Shadow all your hopes
 with love
Live your life without
 a doubt
Outside in and inside out
Pray for guidance from
 above
Pray for guidance from
 above
Shadow all your hopes
 with love
Never be afraid, never
 be afraid
Pray for guidance from
 above
The closing of a chapter
The opening of a door
Brings forth life
Where there was no life
 before

C. "The Reflection"

(instrumental)

Foreword

If the song I sing for you
Could fill your heart with joy
I'd sing forever

Let the love I have for you
Live within your heart,
And beat forever

So I've gone away
But not forever*

From the time I first met Dennis Wilson, he acted as if he would be immune forever from any of the consequences of his actions. Denny lived constantly on the edge, and I always knew deep in my heart that he'd never die of old age!

Somehow I think that if Dennis knew about this book, he'd say in his own character-istic way, "What's the big deal all about? Get along with your lives". Then when he found out that Brian Berry, Paula Haynes, Chris Kable, Alice (BBFUN) and so many of the others who truly loved him were taking part, he'd probably say, with tears swelling in his eyes, "it's about time we set the record straight". Yes, DW, it certainly is.

If, like they say, the early sixties were merely an extension of the fifties — innocent, exciting, upbeat — living for the moment and not looking ahead to tomorrow — then, perhaps, The Beach Boys were also an extension of that same idyllic feeling. No other American group in the history of rock so epitomized an era, nor did any other group come so close to capturing youth. They related to us because they were us. And if there is a way of summing up our musical experience during that period of our lives — before Viet Nam, before Watts, before JFK and Dallas, before, as Don Henley would later sing, "the end of the innocence", we could come to only one conclusion: The Beach Boys.

If you were to ask a hundred, a thousand, a million fans, "Who best epitomized the true essence and spirit of The Beach Boys", I'm **certain** that the answer would be unanimous, "Dennis, Dennis, Dennis".

In those early years, when the Boys were heralded as "America's #1 Surfing Band", it was Denny who was the only true surfer; later, during the "car song" period, it was again Denny who was the drag racer in his bright yellow Cobra. As The Beach Boys evolved into an internationally acclaimed vocal-instrumental group, Dennis, too, began to play a more creative role — as a songwriter, producer, and lead singer — all this in addition to providing the charisma, magnetism, and visible energy on stage. He was irresistible to the girls and electrifying to the entire audience.

When the other members of the group would often talk about solo projects, it was Dennis who gave us "Pacific Ocean Blue" — and, although it was not a huge commercial success, it helped give us an insight into a Dennis that few had anticipated or even believed existed.

Looking back to May 24, 1963 when I first booked the group and came to know Denny, it is often hard to realize that so much has happened. No one imagined that the group, and the music that they so unselfishly shared with the world, would last four decades; that they would continue to tour the world and consistently "sell out" concert halls and arenas; that their music would be the subject of sociology studies, a ballet troupe, numerous retrospectives, TV movies, books, commercials, and countless "sound-a-likes" — to say nothing of the thousands upon thousands of bands that have been inspired and influenced by their distinctive and revolutionary sound.

To remember The Beach Boys, without remembering Dennis is virtually impossible. For, like I have said, Denny was The Beach Boys. No, not in the sense of detracting from the creative genius of Brian or the rest of the guys, but in the sense that he captured the overall spirit of the group, onstage and off.

Even to this day, often when I think of Dennis tears will come to my eyes, and a special smile will come to my face — for the memories of the times we shared, and the love that he so often extended to a special group of people who stood by him.

Shortly after Denny's death, I received a call from our dear friend Paula Haynes. Paula, as this book will note, is a very special friend to all the Boys, but was particularly close to Dennis. As Paula and I spoke, reliving so many of the wonderful times we had shared with DW, I told her that we should brace ourselves for the sensationalized stories that were sure to come out about him. "They'll talk about the drug abuse, the alcoholism, the womanizing; they'll rehash the Charlie Manson stuff, the ex-wives, and all the rest".

Then, after a brief moment, I added, "but Paula, you and I were fortunate to know the other Dennis — the loving father, the caring, tender side of him. We're the lucky ones, Paula".

So, now, perhaps, in these writings, photos, and remembrances, you too, will have an opportunity to share what a few of us "lucky ones" shared for so many, many years.

In an industry not known for many true or enduring friendships, Denny was my closest friend for over twenty years. We didn't have to talk on the phone every week; we didn't write endless letters; and, sometimes, it was often months and months between our visits. But when we did get together it was like no time had passed at all.

The special bond that existed between Dennis and I was a "once in a lifetime" experience and one that I will cherish for the rest of my life. And when I think of Dennis, as I often do, it is a happy occasion. I was honored to have known this special human being, and that, in the long run, is what life is all about.

Fred Vail

August, 1990
Nashville, Tennessee

Introduction

Two questions may come to the reader's mind upon picking up this book. First, who am I to do such a book, and second, why such a book on Dennis Wilson?

To try to answer the first question I would have to say that my biggest credential is that I am a fan of Dennis Wilson and the Beach Boys. I was listening intensely to them while growing up in Phoenix and Los Angeles in 1964 on up to today. Some people have tried to write about Dennis and the Beach Boys without being a fan first. There is a difference I believe. To be an objective viewer of Denny and the Beach Boys is missing something important. You can look at a glass of water when you are thirsty, but it is not the same as drinking it. The Beach Boys music also becomes a part of you if you allow it to, especially if you were growing up with it and experiencing those same feelings and emotions as in their songs.

Music and art were and still are major parts of my life. As a visual artist and photographer I saw something different and special about Denny that compelled me to want to study and observe him more and more. This leads me to the second question, Why a book on Dennis Wilson?

It is a little hard to try to separate Denny from the Beach Boys and to hold him up as a distinct individual, but this is what I have attempted to do for specific reasons. I have something I've seen in Denny that I'm sure is what drew others to him as well. This is what I want to share. My thoughts and views are not meant to be dogmatic and authoritative, but only a shared observation of one artist's tribute to another. In no way does this body of work mean to imply that it is a definitive and conclusive study on Denny, it is really only a beginning point. Dennis was indeed a multi-faceted, complex person, but one common denominator among his associates who shared with me was his magnetism and impact on people. A phrase I heard over and over was, "I miss him". Denny made a lasting impression on those who met him .

I cannot express enough thanks to the many people who shared with me about Denny, both friends and fans. They helped me with personal stories and with research materials.

One sad note was those who refused help because of their honorable loyalty to Dennis and their distrust of the Press from past experiences. This was a big stigma I had to overcome.

To those who were skeptical about my intentions all I can say now is to judge the book for yourself and to see that we both share the admiration of a truly gifted and unique man.

A lot of the Press has dwelled on the negative, sensationalistic side of Denny's life. I am not trying to deny his excesses, bad judgements, and his tragic downward spiral, but I am deliberately focusing on the other areas that the majority of the Press chose to overlook. This is the 'soul' and 'heart' I see dominant in him.

Does the good outweigh the bad in our lives? Does Grace over-ride Law in the final analysis? I choose to believe so.

Edward Wincentsen

Tulsa, Oklahoma
1990

16

DENNY
REMEMBERED

1

David Leaf's Interview

The following is an interview David Leaf did with Dennis concerning **Pacific Ocean Blue**. The interview was originally published in David Leaf's **Pet Sounds**, Volume 1, Number 3, September 1977 under the title of: <u>Dennis Wilson: It's About Time.</u>

Dennis Wilson is autographing posters for what seems like every radio station in the United States. One after another, his personal assistant calls out the names . . . WABX, WINZ, KOME, KSJO, and on and on.

Finally, his promotional chores finished, Dennis is ready to talk. Lounging against the wall of Brother Studio's back music room, smoking a cigarette and drinking a cup of coffee; it's the first time Dennis has rested all day.

However, the leisure moment is brief and he quickly launches into a discussion of the individual tracks on Pacific Ocean Blue.

"The River Song" A few years ago, I was in the High Sierras walking by this river that was very small and it kept getting bigger and bigger . . . that's the guitar sound on the track. And then thinking, Los Angeles vs. the High Sierras, it just makes me sick to think of what's happening here. That's the lyrical idea; Carl assisted on some of the lyrics. Musically, it came from the river.

The voices on the beginning of the song sound like the whole family. Are they there?
Ninety per cent of those voices are mine.

"What's Wrong?" That was spontaneous; I love that old feel that Brian used to play. I was having an argument with a girl I was living with, and I used to say, "What's wrong with me making my music? What's wrong with me not being here all the time? What's wrong with being a little crazy once in awhile? . . . You spend my money. I think it's funny to watch you do that" . . . "Who Made My Moonshine?" Well, you know who made my moon shine. It's a song about Karen.

"Friday Night" That's another spontaneous song. It's a memory of when I was young and Friday night came. The white punks were out having fun. I am *the* white punk!. . . "Dreamer" is about Christ. Musically, I played the bass harmonica on that; I played practically everything on it.

Thoughts of Karen "Thoughts of You" . . . it was a time when Karen left me, and I thought it was completely over, and I accept that sometimes things *are* over.

"Time" . . . that's about coming home after a tour and floating into L.A. on a 747. I just heard it; I heard the music coming out. Thinking about her . . . just a spontaneous thing. "You and I" is about Karen and myself, that's it.

You wrote those last two with her. Is it painful now to have to live with them being on the album?

And with her gone? Yes . . . (long pause) . . . that's the way it goes. Not painful. I don't regret knowing her or loving her at all. I'm honored to have known her and lived with her. To me, this album is lightweight, has no substance. The next album is a hundred times what **Pacific Ocean Blue** is. It kicks. It's different in a way. I think I have more confidence now that I've completed one project, and I'm moving onto another . . ."Pacific Ocean Blues" - Mike Love wrote the lyrics for that one.

"Farewell My Friend" My best friend died in my arms, and I came to the studio. I knew that he loved the Hawaiian Islands; the song just happened, sort of a happy farewell. It's written for Otto Hinsche, Carl's father-in-law. I carry a picture of him everywhere. When my father died, Pops (Mr. Hinsche) saved my life in a way . . . "Rainbows" is about being happy and being alive.

"The End of the Show" strikes me as being a farewell of sorts.

It is. It's two things. I know that the world is coming to a place now where mankind is going to give up war . . . the old is dying. At the same time, it was when I knew that Karen and I were finished.

I get the feeling that there's a lot of pessimism in the music. Do you see any hope for the world?

Absolutely! I think there are a lot of sick people that need a lot of help . . . people who have to be educated, have to grow. I feel through art . . . it can be a great deal of help, like Brian in the sixties with what he did and what he can do. I wish he would get off his ass and do it again.

I have great faith in life itself. I'm religious, and I'm not religious. I get stoned, and I don't get stoned. I smoke a cigarette, and I don't smoke a cigarette. I live my life, period. I take it as it comes, and I take responsibility for it. I don't think I should judge people, but I think it's time for people to stop fighting. It's such a profound question that a master would have trouble answering it. Maharishi would say, "Meditate." All I say is: "Enjoy life, try to be an example."

Brother Brian *Making music with Brian for all these years, is he the obvious major influence for you?*

Not influence, inspiration. There's a difference. I think musically I'm far apart from Brian. He's a hundred times what I am musically. Our music is different. I think he *has* been a profound influence in my life. If I was to say that I had a master, Brian would be the man I'd say has guided and helped me through everything.

Dual Careers *How do you juggle your two careers?*

They're one. I am a Beach Boy. I am Dennis Wilson. I own the studio; the Beach Boys record here. When they're not recording, I record. When they record, I record with them.

On the last album, it seems that some of the guys weren't there very much.

You're right. Michael and Alan haven't been participating as much as they should have been. But that will change very soon.

Personal Music *What people helped you with the album?*

Gregg Jakobson stood by my side and supported me and assisted lyrically. James William Guercio supports me 100%. He stands behind me completely.

Are you at all insecure with the role of artist and leader?

No. I take full responsibility. I want to be . . . I want to meet with everyone in the field, want it to be different. I think music belongs on a personal level, instead of the mindless corporation ordering the artist "do this, do that, do this." People have to meet, discover, grow, build.

Does it bother you at all to be so honest in your lyrics?

Why? There's no escape from being honest. On the inside, we're always honest. On the outside, we can bullshit. Inside, there's no escape, and I just . . . {those lyrics}, that's how I felt.

It's almost unheard of to be recording your second album before the first one is even released

. . .

One of the ads promoting PACIFIC OCEAN BLUE.

Autograph party at Tower Records, Hollywood, CA
for PACIFIC OCEAN BLUE album 10/77.

They (the record company) call it one, two, three. I just don't stop recording. You're talking to, if there ever was a freak or somebody completely into it, I am home here at the studio or playing music on the road. When I go to the shack that I stay at, I hate it. Music is everything. The stage, recording music, signing autographs, worrying about the airplay, worrying about talking to you, everything. If there was ever a real lover in my life, it'd be Karen Lamm and music. Sounds silly, doesn't it? I just love it. I have so much fun doing it. I want you to come by the studio tonight to watch me record...it's a new approach ...a song called "He's A Bum." Even has a nasty line in there - "he likes to do it on his hands and knees." I know that's terrible but . . .

Autograph party at Tower Records, Hollywood, CA for PACIFIC OCEAN BLUE album 10/77.

Spring of 1968.

Denny the
sportsman.

January of 1968.

Spring of 1968.

2

Denny and His Music

"Music is one of the mediums in the world where you can absolutely involve yourself, emotionally, spiritually, and physically. So what I do is get involved."

— From the article: "Dennis Wilson Surfs Alone"
by Randy Meredith Schlenberg.
Bam Magazine, Sept. 1977

There is a lot to be said about Denny and his own music that was just starting to flower.

Denny loved the creating of music as much as performing it. He loved writing music and he also loved the recording process and the studio. This can be heard on various interviews especially the San Jose, CA radio interviews in 1977.

Here's a quote of importance from Carol Rose, the editor of ROCK MAGAZINE in her article in May 1977 entitled, "Dennis Flies Solo". "I never liked guys who were soloist drummers," he said, "I like the hypnotic rhythm that's consistent — something you can get lost in. It's a perfect feel. The feeling within that rhythm is something I like very much. Then it makes the whole song and program work together. The thing I love about music is, if you play and let go of yourself it becomes timeless."

Denny is seen really getting into the drums on one song in a concert scene from the seventies TV special, "The Beach Boys, It's OK". Also, when they are playing, "Help Me Rhonda", during the instrumental break, Denny gets into some funky keyboard playing, boogie woogie style. Brian, from the second keyboard, even looks over at Denny. It's a great scene. Carl is looking good in the film and the whole group gets rockin' on "The Same Song", but a very different, live longer version than on their album, 15 BIG ONES. This rendition has the Double Rock Baptist Church choir singing with them in a real

Various periods.

gospel groove. Even Brian, with his frightened looking eyes, gradually starts to get into the rhythm as he's directing and leading the song. A smile appears on his face as his heavy frame is bouncing with the beat. Another great moment of the Beach Boys on film!

Denny had a number of great songs within the context of The Beach Boys. Some of them being: "Little Bird" and "Be Still" from the FRIENDS album, "Slip on Through", "Got to Know the Woman", and "Forever" from SUNFLOWER. "Cuddle Up" from CARL AND THE PASSIONS, "Only With You" and "Steamboat" from HOLLAND. And there are others of course, but when PACIFIC OCEAN BLUE came out people recognized Dennis Wilson as someone other than just one of The Beach Boys. They got to see an individual with songs and a talent all his own.

Here is what one reviewer said about Dennis and PACIFIC OCEAN BLUE, "The youngest Wilson brother ... has made an LP that can stand on its own merits as a work of individuality, brooding romanticism and musical integrity." This was written by Mitch Cohen in August 1977 for Phonograph Record Magazine. He goes on to say, "... when he (Dennis) pulls it off, PACIFIC OCEAN BLUE is a unique, offbeat Los Angeles tapestry by a man who's always been more complex than he's seemed. Like his brother, Dennis shows real talent as a minimalist, using brief blocks of musical time to their fullest, compressing a lot of information into a limited space, constantly shifting the sand under our feet."

Another rave again from Carol Rose in her same article, "... Brian isn't the only genius in the group. Dennis' new record gives every indication that he can transcend himself. We're going to see an artist, whose individuality up until now has seen its greatest moment in a group, flower into a performer with a new and unique contribution to make to American music — one that's sure to knock most people off their feet".

Denny's solo album was making a good impression on the critics and public. You can see Denny actually 'mixing' "The River Songs" in the excellent documentary, "The Beach Boys, An American Band". Also, there is a great tribute of Denny towards the end of the video showing various clips of him to the tune of "Forever".

Audree Wilson, the mother of the three Wilson brothers, had a comment on Denny's album that appeared in the official Beach Boys Fan Club newsletter, Vol III, Number 2, May 1978. "I loved it. I think it's esoteric; I think he's very influenced by the classics and jazz. I think it's wonderful. I think he's a beautiful talent and a very latent talent".

Someone may ask, "What did Brian think about the album?" Here is a quote from the book, "The Road Goes on Forever, Legends and Superstars of Contemporary Music" by Phillip Norman. "When my record was finished, Brian was the first to hear it," Dennis Wilson says. "In the middle of some tracks he'd say, "I can't stand this" and walk out of the room. Sometimes he'd laugh. Sometimes he'd cry. I guess he was thinking that he'd seen me grow up as a musician".

Denny's album, PACIFIC OCEAN BLUE, is a unique listening experience. Someone has described his voice on it as "light coming through the fog". Rather than give a critical analysis of the album myself, I prefer to let the reader hear it and make their own judgement.

In regards to other music of Dennis Wilson, I will share information I obtained.

There were some rumors that Denny was going to go into the studio to finally mix his BAMBOO recordings. This was to take place after he kicked his alcoholism.

Christine McVie and Denny mentioned a number of times in interviews that they were going to record an album together. Wouldn't that have been something to hear?

There are also other unreleased recordings of Denny's music, some of it supposedly to be his second solo album entitled, BAMBOO. There is live music from Beach Boys shows. From information I received, there never were any solo concert tours of Denny to go with PACIFIC OCEAN BLUE, although it was planned. There are other various demos and home recordings floating around among collectors. All of it demonstrates the special talent Denny had, and a sad reminder of the music that could have been.

A Dennis Wilson Discography

<u>ALBUM SONG OR SINGLE (Dennis' Contribution)</u>

Little Girl (You're My Miss America)(♦)
Hawaii (From the Album "Surfer Girl) (■)
Surfer's Rule (♦)
This Car of Mine (♦)
Denny's Drums (●, drums)
Auld Lang Syne (From the "Christmas" Album) (spoken message)
The Wanderer (♦)
Do You Wanna Dance (♦)
In The Back of My Mine (■)
You've Got To Hide Your Love Away (♦)
Little Bird (♠,●,♦)
Be Still (♠,●,♦)
Be With Me (♠,●,♦)
All I Want To Do (♠,●)
Never Learn Not To Love (♠,●,♦)
Celebrate The News (♠,●,♦)
Slip On Through (♠,●,♦)
Got To Know The Woman (♠,●,♦)
It's About Time (♠,●)
Forever (♠,●,♦)
Sound of Free (♠,●,♦)
Lady (♠,●,♦)
Make It Good (♠,●,♦)
Cuddle Up (♠,●,♦)
Steamboat (♠,●)
Only With You (♠,●)
Had To Phone Ya (■)
In The Still Of The Night (♦)
Mona (♦)
I'll Bet He's Nice (■)
I Wanna Pick You Up (■)
My Diane (♦)
Angel Come Home (♦)
Love Surrounds Me (♠,●,♦)
Baby Blue (♠,●,♦)
San Miguel (♠,●)
Sea Cruise (♦)

ALBUMS: Pacific Ocean Blue (♠,●,♦)

KEY:

♦-Lead vocal by Dennis
■-Lead vocal partly by Dennis
●-Written or co-written by Dennis
♠-Produced or co-produced by Dennis

Discography, courtesy of Gary Virts.

40

Various periods.

THE BEACH BOYS

THANKS —
Brian Wilson

Hi! Mike Love

Thanks — Al Jardine

Carl Wilson

At the beach.

43

Various periods.

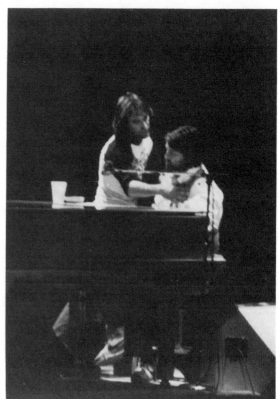

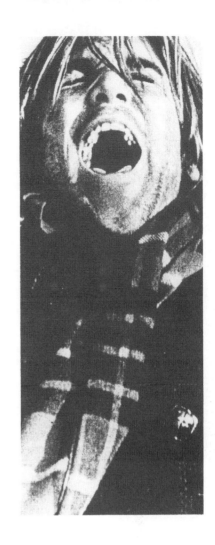

45

3

Words From The Fans

Here is a collection of comments, poems, and articles from fans through a number of sources. Some of these came directly to me, some from other friends, and some from the help of Chris Duffy and her club and publication; Friends of Dennis Wilson. It shows an interesting cross-section of views and reflections.

"It seemed as though by looking at a photo of Dennis or playing a Beach Boys, or Dennis Wilson solo song that it would make everything alright."

— *Gayle Kettler, Michigan*

"I remember Dennis Wilson at the Central Theatre, NJ after a concert in the early seventies. He came out to the limo after the show. He said, "How ya doin' man", after I said to him, "How's it going?"

I remember his handsome movie star looks. After all these years I still will never forget that Dennis Wilson took the time to acknowledge a fan. God Bless the memory of Dennis Wilson."

— *David Schopperth, NJ*

"The first time I heard Dennis Wilson's music it really stunned me. I have always liked the Beach Boys' music; however, I never really distinguished them as individuals.

As a music collector I am always interested in hearing music that I never heard before. Dennis Wilson's solo music was just that, different. His melodramatic style shall always be one of my favorites."

— *Jeremy Moore, Oklahoma*

"I had heard of the Beach Boys, but Dennis Wilson alone? Then I listened to his solo music. He played a wide variety of styles consisting of jazz to gospel. He sounded like a very emotional person.

It has been said people never really die as long as they are remembered. Dennis is remembered."

— *Joyce Moore, Oklahoma*

"I never knew Dennis Wilson. I never saw him perform, but this doesn't mean he hasn't been a part of my life. How do I know Dennis? Through images caught on film and video, through photographs, through words on a printed page, the stories, those who knew him. Most of all through his music because that is where Dennis really lived, and still does.

What matters with any artist is what he leaves behind. Dennis left us music so densely charged with energy and emotion, so passionate, and unprotected, that it speaks with his own voice and says, Live, Live with your whole mind, whole heart, whole soul; feel everything, do everything. Some men live a hundred years, but the essence of their life could be contained in a day. Dennis lived a short life, but the essence of all he felt and experienced could not be contained in a hundred years. He will always inspire me because he showed that sometimes the real danger is being too safe, and the only failure is failing to try.

Jack Kerouac said, "The only people for me are the mad ones, the ones who are mad to live, mad to talk, mad to be saved, desirous of everything at the same time, the ones who never yawn or say a commonplace thing, but burn, burn, burn, like fabulous yellow roman candles exploding".

Rave on, Denny. Forever."

— *Kathryn Kulpa, MA*

Beach Boys Concert - 8/21/75,
Dayton, Ohio - Hara Arena

Beach Boys Concert - 8/21/75,
Dayton, Ohio - Hara Arena

Naturally Denny
by Chris Duffy, President
of Friends of Dennis Wilson

"Denny was very natural. He did everything according to nature's time clock. When anything became too programmed, he had to vanish to some freedom in time, such as: the beach, camping, or scuba diving, Even singing on the stage in super harmony with his friends, fans, and family was a freedom trip to Dennis. He needed to be free, to smile, and this attitude became apparent in his drumming. It was wild and controlled at the same time. Somehow, Denny always came to the end of a song!! Between the beginning and the end, the Beach Boys' drummer was caught in a natural rhythm and beat experience.

Denny's music was natural. His songs of PACIFIC OCEAN BLUE and BAMBOO were not songs to be counted upon in the Hit Parade. He was not that kind of singer. Dennis composed songs from his heart. Most likely, Dennis did not want to put a price on his songs. However, as the song business goes, one who records a song needs to pay the producer and the company. There is more to Denny's songs than just words and rockin' rhythms. The lyrics are poems from his dreams and his music is a blending of sounds created within him. Denny's songs are like prayers or psalms, giving thanks for his blessings. Special messages that are relative to his personal world.

Perhaps, this is why the Beach Boys have not sung one of his songs. They know how special they are and so do FRIENDS OF DENNIS WILSON. He gave us music to remember him and "Music is alive Forever". We can play it over and over again."

— *Chris Duffy, California*

My Favorite Song from Pacific Ocean Blue

"I enjoy listening to many songs on PACIFIC OCEAN BLUE, yet I would have to say that my personal favorite is "Thoughts of You". This song touches me deeply. I love Dennis' wonderfully romantic poetry. I can hear sadness, caring, and passion in Dennis' voice all at the same time. I can even sense his love through the softness of the piano and the quiet - almost silent moments between the verses. I could listen to this song over and over and never tire of it."

— *Carol Tufford, California*

Little Beach Boy

Little beach boy
By the sea,
Dreaming dreams
Of what will be.

Building castles
Made of sand,
Where mermaids dwell
And pirates band.

Little Beach Boy
By the shore,
Your music is
The ocean's roar.

You spend your days
Watching waves
Or exploring lost
Forgotten Caves.

Little Boy
Down on the beach,
Collecting Shells
Within your reach.

This is where
You love to be:
Being as one —
Yourself and the sea.

Little beach boy
Do you have a clue
Of what all life
will bring to you?

With your brothers you'll play
And with them you'll sing,
And bring to the world
The west coast dream.

Then the little boy
Will be a man,
And share his dreams
With all he can.

Of surfing and sailing
And running free;
And your love then, as now,
Will still be the sea.

So play on, little beach boy
'Cause time goes so fast;
And these innocent days
Really don't last.

Too soon they'll be gone
And you'll be all grown,
Taking your place
In the world on your own.

Leaving memories that live on
After each show;
And loved by the people
Wherever you go.

Dear little beach boy
There by the sea,
For Always and ever
You're Special to me.

So dream on of dolphins
And shells and sea — things;
And let them continue —
The world always needs dreams

— *Nancy Lee Amyx, Ohio*

"I saw Denny at the Beach Boys show at the Meadowlands in New Jersey in April 1983. As you can tell by the photo, he wasn't in the greatest of shape at the time. After the first set, the lights were dimmed, and Bruce and Dennis walked on stage, Bruce with an acoustic guitar in hand. They both sat down on stools and with Bruce  strumming, Dennis sang, "You Are So Beautiful to Me". He struggled to get the words out, his voice so gravely that you could hardly understand what he was singing, but we were so close to the stage that you could see in his eyes that he really cared about his fans, and was trying to do the best that he could up there.

I saw him again in June 1983 at Great Adventure and also at Atlantic City on July 4th, 1983, but sitting on that stool, singing his heart out, is how I want him to be remembered."

— *Rick Colville, New Jersey*

Little Help From A Friend

"I spoke with Brian Wilson the other day, while he was autographing his LP at Tower Records in Hollywood. I mentioned the club (F.O.D.W.) and he was very pleased about the whole idea (as you know Dennis was one of the people that "Brian Wilson" was dedicated to). Brian told me that "One For the Boys" was the oldest piece of music (although I think he might be mistaken, as "Little Children". . . aka "They're Marching Along" . . . dates from 1977) and was done as a "spiritual thing" for Dennis more than the Beach Boys. He also told me that he, Brian, did all the vocals on that track as well as on "Love And Mercy".

— *Tom Caton, California*

"Denny Wilson will always be remembered in my heart as the man he was, a musician who loved to entertain. A man who was down to earth, caring, sensitive, and loving."

— *Tawnya Barber, Oklahoma*

Goodbye Dennis

You've given me so much happiness
I listen to your voice and it calms me
You seem like someone I'd love to know
As I watch you weave your magic wand

I could never write songs the way you do
But it makes me feel good to share the beauty
You write masterpieces of nature and
Your love of the sea

I wish you could've stayed awhile longer
We were just getting to know you
If we had only known that you had
So little time

Please forgive all those around you
Who hurt you or forgot you were there
You are such a gentle soul
And many people took you for granted

Now that we can't see you again
We have all learned
You made mistakes like everyone else
But celebrity took its' toll

You were the one who sang the words
Even in the most breathless moments
You'd reach out and touch our souls
But it was you who was so Beautiful.

— ANONYMOUS

"Back in 1964, I was a high school sophomore who enjoyed the Beach Boys' music very much. Their music projected in me a feeling, one which words cannot adequately do justice. It was a feeling inside my inner soul, one which radiated a certain youthful spirit, an intangible spirit, a warm glow.

Sure, I liked the Beatles and the Stones, but the Beach Boys' music unlocked in me a different awareness and sense of belonging to a youthful culture. Their songs stood for something and really meant something: sunshine, convertibles, young tanned girls, and most of all, a feeling of being young.

Now, if Brian Wilson could write a song today with that same wonderful spirit he effortlessly did back then, well then maybe, for one day I could feel like a teenager all over again. "

— *Neil Schoenholz, New Jersey*

"At first I couldn't believe it — not my Denny! I didn't think I could ever feel so helpless and lost. I know he will always be with me. I feel his spirit when I sing. I could never explain how he touched me so … I'll just go on loving him, and listening to him, and maybe one day, I'll meet him."

— *Nanette Comstock, Michigan*

"I first met Denny backstage after a April 1, 1975 show in Kentucky. He made me feel like I was his best friend at that moment.

What I remember most was that I went back to ask him a few questions and it ended up with me answering Denny's questions like; what was life like in Kentucky, things like that.

I saw him again after shows in late March 1979 and early April 1979. He remembered my name at the second show. Again he was very polite and very nice. A guy with a big, big heart.

Saw Dennis again in August 1980. I had a knee injury and was in a total leg cast. I could not put weight on my knee. I was miserable. It was over 90° that night at the show, plus I could not sit down because my leg wouldn't fit between the rows of seats. So the stadium officials let me stand on my crutches up by the stage. During the show the group made a few comments about my cast, then during the slow segment of the show Dennis came over and talked a few moments. He wanted to know about my accident and he signed my cast before he left. Boy, I totally forgot about my misery! He put a smile on my face and a glow in my heart that evening, and you know … he still does to this day when I think of him or listen to his music."

— *Stephen Mayo, Kentucky*

Photo: Annie Leibovitz

66

Music Awards rehearsal.

68

Music Awards.

Christine McVie, Lindsey Buckingham, Carl Wilson.
Spring, 1980 - Lexington, KY

Beach Boys Concert - 8/21/75,
Dayton, Ohio - Hara Arena

New Year's Eve Party.

4

"THE DRUMMER WITH THE KNACK WAS A SURFER"

...By Domenic Priore

(Editor's note:)

Those who are acquainted with Domenic Priore's style of outspoken writing on The Beach Boys and Pop Culture will find his usual flair of wit, biting oratory, and controversy within this piece written especially for this book. The opinions expressed in this article are those of the writer and do not necessarily reflect my own, however I do consider Domenic a major voice to be heard today concerning the Wilson Brothers, and the The Beach Boys. His highly acclaimed book: Look: Listen: Vibrate: Smile! (in the Dumb Angel Gazette series) is a must for any serious fan of The Beach Boys and for anyone remotely interested in rock and roll history. Flipping through the booklets in a number of Capitol's newly released Beach Boys CD's, you will see Domenic's writings and research along with that of David Leaf's. Enough said ... *Ed Wincentsen.*

There are a lot of things one can say about Dennis Wilson. Having never known the man himself, I can only go on what it is that I got out of him. Actually, I may have never known Dennis, but I did know a lot of punks down here in Southern California like him. In the mid-sixties, there was this ultra-hip Mod flick by the title of "The Knack (and How To Get It"). Dennis Wilson exemplified better than anyone what it was to "have it". The film title is misleading. There are those who can try to achieve "it", and others who may come close to getting "it" ... Come on guys, there ain't one of you who doesn't know just what it is that I'm talking about ... try as you may, there is really no way that you can actually "obtain" the magic of personal magnetism that your local Casanova seems to have been born with ... but hey, every neighborhood seems to have one, right? None other than Dennis Wilson, from Hawthorne, California, in the eyes of the world and in the spirit of Brian Wilson's most popular records, could best define "it".

Now, bein' a punk has a lot to do with it. It's certainly the reason chicks perceive you as the kind of rebel that just might be fun to ride with ... and Dennis rode 'em all (or at least as much as he could). It would be a damn lie to say that Dennis Wilson didn't groove with his own nature. But it's not that easy, not a bowl of cherries as most of us outsiders can tend to believe. There are rights that you have to earn, and fights, attitude and will have everything to do with it. Man, Dennis played THE DRUMS ... did you hear me, man HE PLAYED THE DRUMMMMSSSSSS!!!!!!! You people really don't get to hear those on the radio, or in music today at all. The recording engineers have taken them away from us by trying to put a microphone on every damn inch of the kit, until they decided it wasn't worth the time and just took human beings from behind the kit, and faked a beat on a keyboard instrument: I'll say it again: DENNIS PLAYED THE DRUMS !!!!! There are reasons a kid is drawn to play the drums. The kind of guy Dennis Wilson was, he did more than revel in the primitive desire to beat things for a loud, clean noise; he pursued it to the tenth power! And there wasn't a better avenue than surfing music to live it out with ... I mean, listen to "Wipe Out" by the Surfaris sometime, then you'll get the picture. At a Surfer Stomp in the early 60's, the dancing was like a primitive sabbatical rite. There was something "like a wild Indian" about it for sure. Dennis Wilson took to this spirit and added his appeal, his hair, his physique, his sway, his bravado, and his zest for living. He was a guy who was used to gettin' all sandy and salty from the surf on a daily basis, and that adds a devil-may-care elegance to your style for sure. He took this unassuming style to the T.A.M.I. Show in late 1964 and helped to make that the greatest filmed rock-n-roll concert of all time. He also brought it to "Shindig" and "The Ed Sullivan Show" ... check it out, every time Dennis is on camera, the wild screams hit peak levels ... that's because the chicks in the studio audience are watching the monitors, and they had every reason

92

to scream, because Dennis gave it to them ... he knew what excited them, and you could just <u>witness</u> how the screams of Beatlemania triggered the rabid energy in Dennis' full-throttle drumming attack ... Dennis took those screams and stepped on the gas! He knew it was him, Brian & Carl on instruments, and they knew what it was to keep up with him. Perhaps this and no other combination of players should legally bear the right to be known as "The Beach Boys", because, let's face it, no other combination in the world could be that inherent to hyperactive motion, to rock 'n' roll in its truest form; High-Spirited! I can accept no other form as the real thing, because the real thing, it's too darn clear, is too darn good!

Unfortunately, Dennis' highly talented rhythm section partner (and brother), Brian, was overwhelmed with being responsible for songwriting, production, singing and performing everything that made The Beach Boys a viable artistic act. Therefore, he had to drop the least necessary element to coming up with fantastic records and quit "the road". The Beach Boys would never be the frantic rock 'n' roll act they were with the three brothers hittin' it. However, there is a place for musical stretching and growth, and as Brian's music became more complex and intricate, so did Dennis' drumming style on stage. By now, he was no longer on the records, but it's as if he was translating, in performance, the shifts and moods that Brian was layin' on the music world by sibling telepathy. More than the rest of the group, Dennis held Brian's feeling on stage in check, by exalting the cool that was feeding between himself and the master. With Carl's graceful voice keeping the sing-ing together, the road version of The Beach Boys were able to please a more scrutinizing audience for the next 6 years, while Brian laid down everything from PET SOUNDS and "Good Vibrations" to FRIENDS and "Break Away" out in Hollywood.

It was during this creative time that Dennis was able to get his feet wet in the areas of composition and production as well, and on FRIENDS, Dennis came up with "Little Bird", a rather unassuming title, but nonetheless a record that showed best the true values in the free spirit of Dennis Wilson. He was the type of guy who dug surfing, skin and scuba diving, fishing, the drums, hot rods, dune buggys, gardens, beautiful girls and skateboards the same as he dug music in itself, and it's here where it all begins to come together in his art. Dennis had been singing lead on some of the better Beach Boys album tracks over the years, as far back as "Little Miss America" on SURFIN' SAFARI, and right on through to "Surfer's Rule", "This Car Of Mine", "The Wanderer", "In The Back Of My Mind" and "Do You Wanna Dance", bringing a conviction to the vocals that could hardly be equaled in terms of a west coast "show me" grit. Just check out the line, "tight" in "Kiss Me Baby" ... why do you think Brian chose Dennis to sing that one part, that one word? In "Little Bird", it all comes together in one song, and that's Dennis. From here on in, there are probably more Dennis Wilson creative outbursts than can be accurately accounted for in the pages of a photo book, but let me tell you the highlights ... take for example the flip side of their last Capitol 45, "Celebrate The News", (his most fully realized recording with the group), or on 20/20, where Dennis had the spine tingling "Be With Me" and the full-force feeling of "All I Want To Do", which more than simply states the honesty of man's emotion ...

> "All I Want To Do With You, I Just Want To Make Some Love To You
> Come on Baby! I Just Want To Do It With You!"

Dennis never lost track of the primitive, even in the dippy existence of 1969.

But that was only a start. On SUNFLOWER, Dennis <u>and</u> Brian carry the album, a record full of wonderful harmonies, great songs, brilliant production and a <u>"true"</u> Beach Boys/ Wilson Brothers spirit. Believe it or not, Dennis, Brian and Carl were artistically vindicated on this record much in the same way that they proved their greatness on stage during 1961-1964. "Forever" will stand as perhaps Dennis' most famous ballad, "Slip On Through" his best example of songwriting exuberance. The cruncher is "It's About Time", and the best way to describe what happened here can be seen on the T.V. special "Good Vibration from Central Park" from 1971 ... it's here that Dennis performs "Forever" with the group live, a stirring and heart warming rendition indeed. It's followed by Carl busting into "It's About Time" ... their performance of this number in front of an excited, post-Woodstock/New York City throng, and the crowd's impulsive reaction to Dennis' new music is absolutely astounding ... when the group launches into "I Get Around" as a finale, it is anti-climactic.

But in no way was Dennis selfish as a member of The Beach Boys. SUNFLOWER is full of the majesty that could only come from the touch of Brian Wilson. This is the last great Beach Boys album, and Dennis always knew how to let the master do his thing. For Dennis, to instill his feet all over the work of the group, as has been the case for the other members in more recent times, would be sacrilege (as it <u>IS.</u>) Therefore, his greatest personal achievements remained just that: He carried his muse and boundless creativity into solo recordings, which began to reach fruition in 1970. His first record was only released in Europe because he wanted to see what it would be like as an artist in Europe. "Sound of Free" and "Lady" were recorded with a member of The Beach Boys touring group, Daryl Dragon, known as "Captain Keyboard". It was with Dragon that Dennis began to chart a wonderful solo course in unreleased recordings such as the chilling "All My Love", "I've Got A Friend" and "Barbara", which are only the tip of the iceberg as to what could possibly be the greatest missing treasure chest in the musical chronology of Dennis Wilson, the artist. It is certain that in "Lady" and "Barbara", we are dealing with some of the most beautiful and emotional music that ever came from the wide scope of The Beach Boys canon, and that's saying quite a lot from a group that brought us PET SOUNDS... but that isn't all, and it's a real crime if someone doesn't do something about these tapes so that all of those in love with such a landmark record can hear the beauty in these prime-era recordings of Dennis Wilson. During this time, Dennis' voice was at a timbre that was the perfect realization of his artistic potential. By PACIFIC OCEAN BLUE, his singing had gone through some major changes, and the vocal stylings of his unreleased early 70's recordings were never matched again. The cadenza at the end of "Barbara" is enough to tell the true story of Dennis Wilson's artistic peak, and we'll be waiting to hear a collection of this material when a label with some brains and sensitivity to this great man and his many fans gets on the ball and releases a few definitive compilations of his work.

In the meantime, his fans can search the swap meets and record stores for a copy of either CARL & THE PASSIONS: SO TOUGH or PACIFIC OCEAN BLUE. On the former are two examples of intended Dennis Wilson "solo" recordings from the early 70's, "Make It Good" and "Cuddle Up". It's on "Cuddle Up" in which The Beach Boys manage to achieve their most angelic sound of all time, with Dennis as your warm and loving host. PACIFIC OCEAN BLUE, the first "official" solo album from a Beach Boy (unless you count PET SOUNDS) more than impressed every level of rock writer and critic, and therefore was in good company with the 1988 BRIAN WILSON album as the only Beach Boys related release since SUNFLOWER to receive such just critical praise. My theory is that there is good reason for this reality: artistically, The Beach Boys have been D E A D since their popular revival behind the strength of Capitol's ENDLESS SUMMER reissue package. Since that time, the attempts at creativity within The Beach Boys have been something less than half-hearted, and they're still cruisin' by their own admission. It was PACIFIC OCEAN BLUE that addressed this reality in the face of stagnation. The strength of "The River Song", "Rainbows" and the many others on this magnificent album are living proof that The Beach Boys sure have wasted far too many years as a traveling carnival, and have repressed the continuation of the music that could have come from

Brian and Dennis Wilson.

It's not as if the will for it to happen didn't exist. On the unreleased ADULT/CHILD album, the simple, pure joy of "It's Trying To Say" may best sum up what this kind of creative continuation could have meant. The unreleased MERRY CHRISTMAS FROM THE BEACH BOYS features a tremendously moving Dennis Wilson performance in "Holy Evening". By 1981, it must have felt so futile for both Dennis and Brian that they actually began to hold recording sessions together, with Dennis producing this time, and Brian going for the guts in his music on a demo of "Oh Lord", that for the trained ear, has to be the most unrestrained emotional and spiritual plea that I've ever heard from Brian. With Dennis' intense keyboard "answer" moods backing it up, you can hear exactly what the true artistic direction of The Beach Boys might have been had the two most talented members of the group been able to penetrate the surface of the living circus that

surrounded them. When Brian and Dennis were laying this down, you were probably happy that "The Beach Boys Medley" was on the charts. To Bad, but even more that that: What A Shame.

It must have been even more frustrating for Dennis, though. There were times when he could only do the logical thing, and that was to beat up Mike Love right on stage! A lot of people would like to have seen this happen; Dennis, in his integrity made it happen! In 1979, when The Beach Boys obviously didn't have enough good material for their debut album on a new label, CBS. So they nicked some of the better stuff ("Baby Blue" and "Love Surrounds Me") that was slated for Dennis' proposed second solo album BAMBOO. His other great works from that project ("Companion", "Wild Situation", "He's A Bum" and more) remain unreleased to this day, having

Fleetwood Mac's Christine McVie & Beach Boy's Dennis Wilson visit KHJ Studios. Pictured left to right: McVie, KHJ's Bobby Ocean, Wilson, & KHJ's Program Director Chuck Martin.

96

never been realized as a part of their original project. This kind of frustration played hard on Dennis, who was being artistically abused by The Beach Boys in much the same way that they have been abusing Brian since PET SOUNDS. Remember, it was Dennis, who in 1966 spoke the classic line about SMILE: "In my opinion, it makes PET SOUNDS stink, that's how good it is". 17 years of battling the backwards artistic negligence of The Beach Boys became too heavy of a cross to bear for a man of the caliber of Dennis Wilson. I'll put it to you straight: Dennis got wasted, lost his voice, lived awhile in distressing futility, and drowned in his beloved Pacific Ocean at the end of 1983, where The United States of America gave him an honorable burial at sea. Such an honor is usually reserved for members of the militia. However, no American nor planet earth civilian could possibly come to represent the free spirit of the open sea in the eyes of the world more fully than Brian Wilson's inspiration in writing the great rock 'n' roll records that became internationally accepted as such by The Beach Boys: The reckless innocence and wild abandon that was Dennis Wilson.

...By Domenic Priore

BL: Karen Lamm Wilson

All photos
Summer, 1978
Pine Knob, MI

104

Top: Jennifer and Dennis Wilson at Gage's 1 year Birthday Party, Sept 1983.

Bottom: Left to Right: Carl, Jennifer, Dennis, Michael, and Gage Wilson, at same party.

5

Denny's Children

Denny was married a number of times and had children with all but one of his wives. In the next chapter, Fred Vail tells a story about Denny's love and devotion as a father. These unedited writings by all of his children, except Gage (who was only one year old at the time of Denny's death), confirm the love he had for his children.

A VERY SPECIAL FATHER
Jennifer Beth Wilson

My father once told me that love could not be begged, borrowed or stolen. Only given.

I may not have been able to spend as much time with my father as I would have liked to, but the time that I did spend with him was the most valued a child could have.

He was very special to me ... as I know I was to him.

I wish that he could have been here to see his first grandson, Matthew being born. He would have been so proud.

I respected my father with all my heart and soul. I watched as he constantly gave away all that he had to others, asking nothing in return but the satisfaction they received from what he gave them.

I only wish I could have spent more time with him. To tell him how very much I loved him.

I know that my Dad is at peace now, and that puts my mind at ease.

I love you Dad.

MY BEST FRIEND
by Scott Wilson

I'm so happy to have the opportunity to share a few words about my father with you. I would like to say that he wasn't only a good father, but he was also the best friend I've ever had. His problems weren't so very different than those of millions of other people.

Growing up I had the best father a boy could dream of. We spent a lot of time together. Sailing, surfing, fishing, camping and traveling around. Everything was special and everyday brought a new adventure.

I remember an outing at Salton Sea, California. Dad was going to buy a racing boat. We took it out for a test run. I remember it went very fast. Then, without warning, the boat's steering mechanism broke and the boat leapt out of the water, shifting direction unexpectedly.

I flew out of the boat into the water. I was wearing a lifevest but the force of the turn sucked me out of the jacket and plunged me into the sea where I rapidly sank below the surface.

Dennis was unaware at first of what had happened. But quickly noticed I was not in the boat and jumped over the side into the water, diving under the surface trying to find me. Finally, after what seemed like many minutes he made a last attempt to reach me under the muddy water. He thought I was lost forever. At that moment he somehow bumped into me and managed to grab me and pull me out and up onto the boat.

He performed artificial respiration and got me breathing again. I wish I could have been there for him.

He will always be in my heart. He was a very big part of my life and I treasure the memory of the times we shared.

It's nice to see, through this book, that a lot of people cared for Dennis and want to share the good things about him.

Photo,

I love you Dad.

Scott, Dennis, Jennifer Wilson

108

Michael, Dennis and Carl Wilson

Ode To My Father

My father was an ocean man and loved to get wet.
He would stay until 5:30 to watch the sun set.
And when I went to his house he had a party or celebration;
But if not one of those, it would be a combination.

My father was a joker; he would always mess around.
He could probably make you laugh even all year round.
My father was like a king at the round table,
He was also a broken chair, very unstable.

My father was full of surprises, he was very very funny.
He got my little brother a snake and me a baby bunny.
My father was into music; he became a famous drummer.
Soon he came out with a hit record; it was called "Endless Summer".

My father was so strong he had the power of a gun.
When two drummers played, he was louder as one.
Soon it was time for him to take his last breath;
But I think he understood he had to face something called death.

Carl B. Wilson
1986

Michael, Barbara (Denny's 2nd Wife) and Carl Wilson - 1987.

I remember my father as a very loving man who had a unique sense of humor and a fine taste for cars. I wouldn't consider him as a family man, but he sure did a good job as my father.

Whenever I saw him I always had high hopes. I used to think about what made Dennis so different. I felt that no matter who he was with, they were always happy to be with him. Dennis was a very well-liked man who had a one of a kind personality.

I loved my father very much. I remember some days when he would take me and my brother all over in his red hot Ferrari. I remember one time when my father was with my older brother Mike in one Ferrari and Karen Lamm and I were in another Ferrari. We raced up to Big Bear Lake in the night. My dad seemed to have taken the lead until sometime later when Karen and I passed him as he was being ticketed for speeding. Karen decided to get something to eat so we stopped off at this little Mexican restaurant. About a half hour later, Dennis and Michael walked in the restaurant. Dennis was so irritated that he grabbed my burrito and inhaled it in one bite.

I miss times like that. I hope that people will love and remember Dennis for the wonderful person he was. I love you and miss you very much.

Love always, your son, Carl.

11-8-90

Left to Right: Gage, Michael, Dennis and Carl Wilson at Gage's 1 year Birthday Party - Sept 1983.

When I was asked to write something about my father it was very hard for me to think of what to say. He was someone that I never really saw very much of; nevertheless, when I did see him, he always tried his best to be a good father.

I hated going home without him; I needed him with me. There are so many things I wish I could have experienced with him. So many things I wish I knew about him. Growing up I held onto every piece of information concerning him and cherished it.

I was a baby when I lived with my father and sadly enough my memory can stretch only so far. He had many problems that as a kid I never saw, I only got his love and happiness. The best memory I have of my father is when he took my brother Carl, and me, and my friends to Fatburger on LaCienega. It would be such a good time. He had a beautiful Rolls with a rumble seat. We would eat our lunch under the trees in the little park. I also remember going to Beach Boy concerts. They were fun but they just didn't last as long as I wanted them to.

I wish my dad and mom could have raised me. I have never had a real father figure and I have missed that throughout my life.

With love always, your son, Michael

11-8-90

Houston, TX - The Summit. Al Jardine receiving a kiss from a fan, and Dennis.

Top: Beach Boys 20th Aniversary Party - Hollywood, CA

Left to Right: Betty Collignon, friend, Trish Roach, body guard, Dennis,
Alice (BBFUN, Beach Boys Fan Club), Brianne & Ed Roach.

Bottom: Christine McVie, Sharon Smith and Dennis - 1980.

6

Friend's Recollections

Denny has been overlooked in the press regarding his big heart. The press chose to focus on the negative and bad times of Denny, the sensational side rather than the warm hearted person he was. Here are recollections of his friends and associates who have a strong sense of loyalty to his memory.

BRIAN BERRY

Brian Berry was a photographer who's work can be seen on a number of The Beach Boys tour books and record albums. He so generously, allowed me to use his photos of Denny which comprise the majority of photos in this book. He is still a close friend to The Beach Boys today.

Brian shared with me the following story of Denny early in The Beach Boys career. Denny liked cars, boats, motorcycles, and anything that could go fast. He use to drag race at some of the places outside of Los Angeles. One of the places where he raced, under a different name, was run by someone who is now an editor of a car magazine. This editor, at that time, once asked Dennis why he used a different name and Denny replied, "My dad would kill me if he ever found out".

Brian Berry also recalled that once at a later concert with The Beach Boys, he and Dennis were in a conversation backstage at a college or university when a young co-ed came up and was saying something to Denny. Dennis became very enraged that she should interrupt them and said some very rude things to her. She said she was sorry for interrupting them and left with tears in her eyes. Brian reprimanded Denny for what he did and Denny said that he was right. Denny then ran off to find the girl and to apologize.

Soon Denny and the girl returned. Denny had his arm around her and they were talking like two long lost friends .

HAL BLAINE

Hal Blaine, for those who don't know who he is, is a recording session drummer who has the record of being the world's most recorded musician. He has drummed on some the biggest hit records in music. Some of the artists he has recorded with are: The Mamas & The Papas, The Byrds, John Denver, The Beach Boys, Simon and Garfunkel, Elvis Presley, Frank Sinatra, and the list goes on and on. Hal also has a book out about his experiences in the music world published by MixBooks.

Hal was so kind and gave me these reflections.

"I worked a number of days with Denny on The Pacific album (PACIFIC OCEAN BLUE). Three or four cuts. Denny was an intensely good producer. He knew exactly what he wanted and knew how to get there ... I was most impressed with Denny's piano playing. There was a great Mexican restaurant across the street from Brothers studio and Denny took me there on several occasions. (Also, during the making of that album, his foot was in a cast. He had stepped on a jagged coke bottle in the sand while on the beach. He was so prone to accidents).

We had a lot in common in that we both were riding motorcycles during that period of our lives. (I've given mine up). He had a full blown chopper, mine was a standard 750 Hondamatic, fully dressed, so we came from different biking backgrounds. Mine was very controlled and designed for comfort. Denny's was made for speed, very loud and

118

very uncomfortable. His bike was a sign of his life, fast and reckless, live for today for tomorrow may not come. Ironic isn't it?

We each had yachts, mine a power boat, twin diesel, his a beautiful, very quiet sailboat (the Harmony). Strange again. This time I needed the speed and power, he wanted the South Seas feeling of freedom. I gave up my boat not long after Denny died just a few docks away. He had gutted the interior of his boat and made it a one room, huge salon. Denny was well known in the Marina."

Here is an excerpt from Hal's book:

I am often asked what Dennis Wilson's feelings were about me playing the drums. After all, he was the group's drummer. Dennis and I were good friends. He admired and respected my technique, and Dennis was no fool. The popularity of The Beach Boys was paying for all of his whims — motorcycles, boats, women and fast cars. He was living the good life and I don't think that he really wanted to be in the studios as much as in the early days. But in later years, Dennis became very involved in the Brothers studio complex.*

More things that Hal shared with me, "We were all on a huge rock and roll show in Hawaii back in the sixties ... The Beach Boys were so loved in Hawaii. Denny was the first to appear on a motor scooter and off they went to rent scooters and go sight-seeing ... these were wonderful reflections of the kids ... they were all super nice to me and the rest of the wrecking crew (the other studio musicians with Hal)."

*Excerpt from, "Hal Blaine and The Wrecking Crew". Used With Permission from MixBooks. © 1990

FRED VAIL

Fred Vail wrote the Foreword for this book. For a very good account of Fred's history with Denny and The Beach Boys, be sure to see David Leaf's excellent book: "The Beach Boys and the California Myth", later just called: "The Beach Boys". If you don't have a copy, find one! This is required reading for any Dennis and/or Beach Boys fans! If you can't find one, see the ad for RockAway Records in the back of this book. They have them.

In a nutshell, Fred was the first concert promoter to headline The Beach Boys in 1963. After the success of their first show together, (see poster), Fred became part of The Beach Boys booking process called American Productions. Fred also worked in other areas within the Beach Boys during the years around the SUNFLOWER period. He in particular formed a close friendship with Dennis.

Fred recalled these stories: He had health problems in school with a skin condition. If he bruised or cut his skin accidently, he would have a much more serious injury than normal. Denny knew about this and always watched our for him and his health in general. On one occasion, Fred visited Denny when The Beach Boys were scheduled to have a show aboard the Queen Mary docked in Los Angeles. Fred was spending the night aboard Denny's yacht, the Harmony, and it was a rather cold January winter evening. Fred didn't have a warm shirt, so Denny took off his thick flannel shirt and told Fred to wear it. Denny always the watchful friend!

Fred confirmed the story that Denny was indeed a devoted father to all his children. An absent father, perhaps, but still a father that was truly concerned with the welfare of his children.

Late in 1969 or early 1970, Dennis was up in Canada with The Beach Boys during the period Fred was their manager. During their tour, Dennis received a long distance phone call from his ex-wife that one of their children was missing. This was during the Manson days and Denny had received a number of threats. The call put Dennis in a state of panic. Dennis wanted Fred to charter a plane so he could go immediately to California to help. Since they were up in a smaller, remote city in Canada, an evening charter plane would have cost around $6,000.

Fred found out that they could save thousands of dollars by taking a charter plane to another larger city, then getting a commercial flight to Los Angeles. However, Dennis didn't want to waste any time and was prepared to fly out to California at any expense. Just then they received news that everything was OK and their child was found safe and sound, just a big mix up. Fred said this account always showed him that Denny was a loving father.

In 1980, Fred Vail and a partner took over a failed recording studio in Nashville. They became successful with the studio and during a concert date The Beach Boys had in Nashville, Fred invited them to an open house along with other guests from the music industry. As always, there are lots of things going on with The Beach Boys and only Mike and Bruce stopped over for a short while. Dennis though, came and stayed throughout the evening, meeting guests, signing autographs, playing the piano, and just helping Fred in general. Denny, going the extra mile for Fred.

Fred Vail's poster of the first major Beach Boys Concert.

Fred Vail at Denny's Venice, CA beach house - 1977. Denny was excited about playing some of the early mixes of PACIFIC OCEAN BLUE for Fred.

CHRIS KABLE

Chris Kable was Dennis Wilson's secretary and worker with The Beach Boys and Brothers Studios. (See her letter to the fans in the BBFUN (Beach Boys Official Fan Club) newsletter. Chris emphasized Denny's big heart and childlikeness, she also had a number of stories about Christine McVie and Denny that showed him as the romantic that he was:

"Once Denny had a large heart shaped garden, landscaped in Christine's backyard and revealed it for her birthday party as he sang, "You Are So Beautiful To Me", with the accompaniment of an orchestra. All the guests and friends stood around with candles in their hands."

When Christine and Denny were giving out interviews together I remember reading one in which Christine said, "Denny is introducing me to new things like powerboats and water skiing". This was probably before one experience Christine had with Denny and his "water skiing". Chris Kable told me that once Denny wanted to show Christine what he could do on the water. They were skiing behind a powerboat, Christine only a beginner. Denny was known as a fish in the water, but even what Dennis was suggesting, he was going to do, had them both worried. There was an area of land that stuck out into the water and Denny wanted to show them that he could jump over it while skiing. The land was wide and had jagged, large rocks covering it. The powerboat took off at a high speed and Denny flew over it without a mishap. Both of the girls were rather shook up to say the least, and Chris Kable said that Denny didn't even know for sure if he would make it. He had never attempted it before. Denny always the daredevil!

Christine McVie and Dennis in the recording studio.

Only Over You

music and lyrics by Christine McVie
with special thanks for inspiration to Dennis Wilson

I'm out of my mind
And it's only over you
I'm out of my mind
And it's only over you

People think I'm crazy
But they don't know
Thought love had failed me
But now, they're watching it grow

Angel, please don't go
I miss you when you're gone
They say I'm a silly girl
But I'm not a fool

People say they know me
But they don't see
My heart's your future,
Your future is me

Angel, please don't go
I miss you when you're gone
They say I'm a silly girl
But I'm not a fool

I'm out of my mind
And it's only over you
I'm out of my mind
And it's only over you

Repeat

Chris said Denny was like that, never afraid to try anything new, that Denny was like a child. Immediate, sometimes a bad judge, but trusting of people. She said he would get upset with someone, but would never hold a grudge.

Denny formed a friendship with Fleetwood Mac through his relationship with Christine McVie. Dennis and his brother, Brian, once wrote a song for Stevie Nicks. In San Francisco, Denny had little cakes made for all of Fleetwood Mac on tour. When Denny and Christine McVie would just be hanging out together at Christine's mom's house, Denny would say to her that Christine was his best friend and conscience.

STUART RESOR

Stuart Resor was more an associate of Dennis rather than a close personal friend. Stuart is an architect up in Cardiff by the Sea, California. He owns a completely restored 1946 Mercury "Woodie" wagon that The Beach Boys use for a lot of their concerts and with other promotional things. Stuart first meet Denny in May 1981 at the San Diego Stadium. Stuart would drive The Beach Boys up to the stages of places like baseball fields. (See the photos). At the concert, Stuart drove The Beach boys up to the stage as the crowd of 60,000 fans cheered, however, Denny was late and was not in the Woodie wagon along with the rest of the band. About one third of the way through the concert, some guy went running past Stuart to the stage. It was Denny. They had two sets of drums and another drum-

mer was drumming on the other set. Denny hopped up on the stage and just started playing along with the other drummer. Stuart said Denny had a real heavy beat and that the double-drumming sounded terrific.

Stuart said he didn't see Denny again until the following year, 1982. This time, it was at the Irvine Meadows in Orange County, California, before a concert. The Woodie was in a special security area so people could see it as they came in. Denny introduced his bodyguard as his "friend". Denny was excited about the Woodie and asked lots of questions about it. Stuart asked Denny if he would like to drive it and Denny said yes. Dennis got in and took his shoes off. He had no shirt on, just shorts. Stuart said at this time Denny's

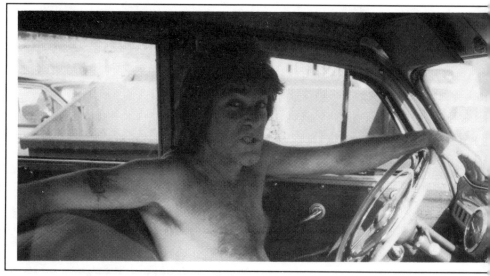

voice was really bad, hoarse sounding and raspy. Stuart asked if he could take a picture and Denny said, "Sure". Here is the photo Stuart took.

Denny took off in the Woodie across the field. The tailgate wasn't closed securely, fell open, and Denny stopped. Stuart walked over, closed it, and got in the Woodie with Denny. Dennis drove around the field for about a half an hour as The Beach Boys

The photo shoot in progress at Mike Love's house.

The three Wilson brothers.

were rehearsing, waving to people and having a good time.

Stuart didn't see Denny again until the next year, 1983, when he was invited up to Mike Love's house for a photo session with The Beach Boys and his Woodie wagon.

Stuart got up there about 9:00 or 10:00 A.M. and met everybody, except Dennis who was late once again. Finally Denny showed up, but was unhappy because People Magazine was also to arrive soon to do an article about The Beach Boys and Denny was afraid that People would put him in a bad light. At that very moment the People Magazine photographers and writers pulled up. Denny was not happy about it and when one of the photographers suggested that they shoot in the Woodie, Dennis said, "Oh, in the woods? That's a great idea". And he immediately took off in the direction of the nearby Cypress trees that surround Mike Love's home and land. The People photographers were seen trying to catch up with Denny as he headed for the "woods". They actually took some photos in the woods.

The following day, The Beach Boys were again playing in San Diego. Then Stuart saw them once more in Ventura. Denny was in great spirits, thanking and greeting everyone. The last time Stuart remembers seeing Dennis, was up on stage, behind his drums motioning for the fans to come up, and even get on the stage (which caused the security people to nearly have heart attacks).

All six Beach Boys together,
(from the photo shoot at Mike Love's house).

PAULA HAYNES

Paula Haynes has a rare illness called morquio syndrome. This is a genetic disorder and strikes people differently. There are only about one hundred cases of it in the United States. Paula is in her late thirties and is only three and a half feet tall. She uses a wheelchair now. Up until the tenth grade she walked, then she had to use crutches. About nine years ago they put her in a wheelchair.

The first time Paula met The Beach Boys was when they were playing in Memphis at the Coliseum for a Thanksgiving concert about sixteen or seventeen years ago. She was working at a radio station then and went to the show with a bunch of the D.J.'s. Because Paula's wheelchair was so small, the concert promoter let Paula sit in the front area by the stage. About half way through the concert when The Beach Boys started playing their greatest hits the crowd all rushed to the front of the stage putting Paula in some danger of being hurt. The promoter saw this and quickly moved Paula under the roped-off security area backstage, or sidestage. Paula couldn't see the show very well from this new location, but there were two small boys there asking her questions about her wheelchair.

Because she couldn't see the show very well, she spent time answering the boy's questions and visiting with them. One of the boys said, "I want my daddy to see this", and he rushed off. Later he came back out and she discovered that his daddy was Al Jardine. The other boy's daddy was Carl Wilson. Soon they were all in a conversation and Dennis came out and joined in.

They all struck up a friendship and The Beach Boys said they would see her the next time they came to Memphis. When they did return, Jerry

Schilling (a friend of Paula's), was their manager. That is how Paula met Dennis and The Beach Boys and would later join them on the road whenever possible. They are still good friends to this day.

One of the first times Paula joined The Beach Boys on the road was in Columbia, Maryland. Paula had a cousin in Washington, D.C. about forty-five minutes from Columbia. Paula and a friend flew up to D.C. to stay awhile at Paula's cousin's house before driving to the concert. However, the forty-five minute drive took them over two hours because they kept getting lost.

When Dennis heard about this, he didn't want to have to worry about them, so he told Jason (who was the road manager) to get them a hotel room for three days and he would pay for it.

There was a mix-up at the hotel and instead of the room being registered under Dennis' alias, it was registered under the name of Dennis Wilson. When Paula and her friends were in the hotel room, they kept getting telephone calls from girls trying to get in touch with Dennis. Paula made a long list of the girl's names and messages. Later Dennis said no girls would every try to reach him at the hotel rooms, so Paula said, "Well, you won't be needing this", and tore up the list in from of Dennis.

Once in Louisville, The Beach Boys were staying at a hotel there, but were playing in another city. They would then return back to Louisville, to their hotel, but not until about 2:00 A.M. At the same time, The Shriners were having a convention in the hotel. Pat Sullivan (a traveling friend) and Paula took a nap then went downstairs about 1:00 A.M. to greet The Beach Boys when they returned. Dennis said he had things to do tomorrow and wanted to visit with Paula and Pat about 3:00 A.M. They sat and talked and played backgammon until 6:00

137

A.M. then Denny said he was getting tired and got up to go to his room. He didn't know about the Shriners being there and when he went out into the hall, one of the Shriners was behind him and started playing a tuba. Denny jumped so high they were afraid he might fall off the balcony. So much for the stories of the rough, tough, trouble-making musicians at hotels.

Denny loved pushing Paula's wheelchair. He'd introduce Paula and say, "Hi, this is my friend Paula. She's short, but I forgive her." He was a pretty good driver, Paula said, except when he would run into Carl or Brian, then he'd just let the wheelchair go off on it's own.

In Knoxville, Pat Sullivan would also act as Paula's bodyguard sometimes. There was a phone call one morning around 6:00 A.M. A deep sounding voice said, "Is Paula asleep?" Unlock the door, I'm bringing something up!"

Pat didn't know who this loud, deep voice was because Denny had disguised it. Pat decided to get up, change into her clothes, unlock the door, and lay back in bed to see who it was. A few minutes later, Denny came in, tiptoeing over to Paula's bedside with a daisy in his hand that he had stolen from a room service tray. He got a glass of water from the bathroom, put the flower in it, and set it down next to her bed and pulled the covers up on Paula.

The following night in Knoxville at their Hilton hotel, Denny decided that he wanted to have a romantic dinner date with Paula. Denny had set it all up with the restaurant for that evening. During the day, Denny went up to visit with Pat to see if she would iron his shirt for the evening. The photo shows Denny in his t-shirt trying to get Pat to iron his dress shirt. However, Pat wouldn't do it.

When Denny went to take Paula up to the restaurant, he told everyone that he couldn't get anyone to iron his dress shirt, and to please forgive him that his shirt was wrinkled. This other photo (both taken by Pat) shows Paula and Denny just before they were ready to go upstairs to the restaurant to the top of the Knoxville Hilton hotel.

When they did arrive, they discovered that one of the local high schools was having their prom there that night. The Beach Boys had just played there so all the kids knew who he was. Paula, was there with Denny in t-shirt and jeans, and all the high school kids were in tuxedos and gowns. Denny kept busy telling everyone about not being able to find someone to iron his shirt and apologizing.

They were there only about fifteen minutes, when Jason, the road manager, came up and said that Denny had to leave because a storm was brewing, and since they were flying to their concert that evening, they would have to leave early to miss the storm.

Their romantic dinner date only lasted fifteen minutes. Pat and their other friend, Honica, were in the hotel room in

139

t-shirts, jeans, and were putting on toe nail polish when they got a call from Dennis saying that there was an emergency and to get up to the restaurant as fast as possible. When they got up there out of breath, expecting the worst, Denny explained, "I wouldn't leave until you got up here. I've got to go. Get over there and eat that food and if you don't spend more than a hundred dollars, I'm going to get mad at you".

Another time, in another city, Denny wanted to serenade Paula. He had Pat come to his hotel room. He had an electric piano there and he wanted Pat to help him move it to Paula's room, but the two speakers were too big for two people to move. Dennis then called some of his friends to help move it, but they thought he was out of his mind. Pat suggested, "Why don't you bring Paula to your room instead?" Denny said, "No", that would spoil the mood. So he didn't do anything.

The next night at the the concert, Denny sang to Paula the song, "You Are So Beautiful". Everything was OK the first verse, but then on the second verse, Denny sang it in his Donald Duck voice. All the crew froze, and Denny laughed and put his towel over his head.

Once in Memphis, when The Beach Boys were playing there, Jerry Schilling, who was their manager at that time, and a former associate of Elvis, had planned to take them to visit Graceland. When they were ready to leave from the hotel, they couldn't find Dennis. Finally, they found him out in front of the hotel picking flowers to put on Elvis' grave.

After they arrived at Graceland, they had just got to the first room when Denny stopped and couldn't go any further because he started crying so hard. Denny went out to the Meditation Gardens where Elvis was buried and stayed out there awhile. He kept crying so hard there that they finally took him out front to comfort him. Paula said that Denny was so moved by things like that.

In Atlanta, Georgia, Jan and Dean were opening for The Beach Boys on tour. This was the first time for Jan and Dean to go back on tour after Jan Berry's auto accident. A bunch of the touring people one day were sitting around in the hotel lobby together talking with Dennis when Jan and Dean came over. Paula was in her small wheelchair and Jan was having his disabled problems from the accident, so they put Jan next to Paula. Everybody said that they were the perfect couple. Then Jan put his arm around Paula and started kissing her and Dennis said, "Hey, wait a minute! Paula's my girl!"

Later, Jan was getting tired and wanted to go back to his room, but was having trouble getting up. Dennis went over to him and said in a gruff voice, "Listen Jan, we've got business to talk over", meaning Paula being his girl. As Dennis did this, he put his arm around Jan, helping him up and to his room. This was Denny's way of helping Jan without Jan knowing it.

One of the Washington, D.C. concerts had a big rainfall that was kind of ruining the mood of the event. It had rained for three days and the place was wall to wall mud.

Paula had been praying for Dennis and his brothers (more on that story in the chapter "Denny, An Observation"). In fact, whenever anyone would come up to Denny and talk about God, Denny would say, "Did Paula Haynes send you?" It was still raining when the other acts were performing. When The Beach Boys got up to play, as they hit the first note, the sun came out. Then over across from

141

the drums, you could hear Denny yell, "Paula's praying again".

Paula remembers the following story as her most moving experience with Dennis. After one of the shows, they had a few days off so Denny had rented a bus to go to a spot to do some fishing. He had the bus all ready, parked backstage so he could leave right after the concert was finished.

Denny had heard that Paula could walk on crutches, but had never seen her. He wanted to see Paula walk. After the show, Dennis took Paula out to the bus and held her up as she walked some in the aisle of the bus. After Paula had taken a few steps on her own, with the aid of the seats along the aisle of the bus, Denny said with tears in his eyes while hugging her, "I'm so proud of you. Don't you ever give up!"

Paula said that this was the kind of person Denny was. That he could be so goofy at times and do some of the dumbest things, but that he was the most loving and tender-hearted person she had ever met. She said he had such a big heart.

Dennis Wilson with Brianne Roach.

Top: Dennis, Carl and Brian at
             RFK Stadium - 6/12/83.
Middle: Bruce and Denny
             Daytona Beach Airport - 4/2/83.
Bottom: Carl, Denny and Mike Love
             Daytona Beach Airport - 4/2/83.

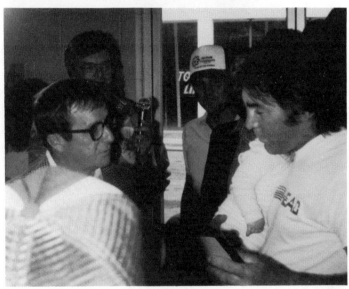

Top Left: Dennis, Shawn (Denny's
4th wife), and Gage.
Michigan, 1983.

Middle Right: Shawn, Dennis

7

Denny, An Observation

"I want to be remembered as warmth. I would just like to make people feel safe. The greatest success in life is to feel I'm something other than a walking, talking machine. I think my favorite feeling of all is feeling something for someone; the feeling of falling in love, the newness of love." His (Denny's) advice to newcomers in an industry fraught with frustrations and tensions is equally as sunny: "Develop your heart."

— Excerpt from: "Dennis Wilson Surfs Alone"
By Randy Meradith Schlenberg
BAM Magazine. September 1977

It is not surprising that Denny advised writers and musicians to develop their hearts. He could be considered an expert on the subject. If there was anything that could be seen in Denny, it was his "heart".

Pat Sullivan reminded me about a characteristic of Denny's. Whenever Denny met someone new for the first time, he would always find some good point about them and mention it as he shook hands. It could be anything from, "You really have beautiful eyes", to, "Great looking shoes!"

This illustration brings to mind the story told to me by Paula Haynes involving children with terminal illnesses who would come to a Beach Boys concert from organizations such as the Make A Wish Foundation. Denny would be there before showtime complimenting them on their good points and giving them undivided special attention. However, after leaving them, Paula recalls, he couldn't hold back the tears because there was nothing else that he could do to help them because of their terminal illnesses. I know if Denny had seen and heard about the story and courage of Ryan White that he would

153

have been another music celebrity there giving friendship and support.

I saw in Denny what some people might call the "heart" and "soul" of a poet; that intense ability to pick up on moods, an empathy for people, and a vulnerable sensitivity.

If Brian Wilson could be compared to the poet William Blake, both for his innocence and trusting childlikeness, then I believe Denny could be compared to the intense flames and passions of people like: the poet, Arthur Rimbaud; the artist, Paul Gauguin; and the writer, Jack Kerouac.

One reviewer of Brian Wilson's solo album said that Brian had a "naive innocence" and I think that is a good description. Dennis, on the other hand, I believe had extremes of his sensitive, quiet side, mixed with volatile intense periods of passion. Like some of these intense poet/artists, I'm afraid Denny also burned brightly for too short a period of time on earth and then left us too early. Many have said that Denny lived more in his short time than others have in a long lifetime. He, himself said he wanted to live life to the fullest.

Chris Kable reminded me that Denny shared the same childlike quality as Brian. Some people told me that Denny was like a big kid, but it was a childlikeness, not a being childish. Van Morrison, the Irish singer and songwriter, has a album entitled, "A Sense of Wonder". I'm sure Denny always had that, a child's sense of wonder. Didn't someone say something like, "Unless you become as a little child ..."?

This brings me to another facet of Denny's personality. Maybe pure speculation? The reader can decide for their self. Paula Haynes told me that every time Dennis heard Carl Wilson's song, "Heaven", from one of Carl's solo albums, that Dennis would cry. What was he crying about? On the BAMBOO album recordings, there is a song entitled, "Carry Me Home" and Denny sings about his fear of dying and about being taken or carried "home".

My editor, Belinda Subraman, had some really interesting thoughts on Denny's song of "Carry Me Home" that I would like to share.

"In the version of "Carry Me Home" that I heard — there was a tearful intensity in his voice. It was not a fear of dying only but a longing for death also in that song — a longing to be with his dad in heaven — "Carry me home to my daddy, carry me home to my Lord." There is a double meaning here — to be with his earth father and his heavenly father. The song is about being utterly tired, utterly tired of the life he is living. In here he predicts his own death — "My eyes are tired. I guess I won't grow old." — "Life is meant to live but I'm afraid to die ... Please God carry me home." He wants the transition to be gentle and easy, the same way he liked to live his life. He's ready but afraid to die. (I would not be surprised if it was one of his very last songs — near the end of his downward spiral.)

Unlike Dylan Thomas he did not want to "rage against the dying of the light."
He wanted to "go gently into that good night."

It touches me deeply each time I hear it."

There are many philosophies and religions of life. I do think it is safe to say that Denny did, and that all of The Beach Boys, believe in some form of a God, whatever definition or actual belief it is. Paula Haynes told me that on a number of occasions she mentioned to Denny that she was praying for him and Denny would say, "Oh, Paula pray for me, but pray for my brothers first because I love them".

Denny stated in David Leaf's interview (which is printed in this book) that his song, "Dreamer" from his PACIFIC OCEAN BLUE album, is about Christ. Also, in the same interview Denny said that his song, "You and I" (again from his PACIFIC OCEAN BLUE album) "is about Karen and myself, that's it". The song, "You and I" is credited as being written by Dennis, Karen Lamm, and Gregg Jackobson. However, towards the end of the song he mentions Jesus and it is vague whether he is talking about Karen or Jesus.

Whatever Denny's beliefs were, I am convinced that he did think on spiritual matters and had a faith that he believed in.

———————————

Lindsey Buckingham was working on his solo album, "Go Insane" when he learned of Denny's death. I was told that Lindsey was so affected by the news that he stopped production on the album to go away to be alone and when he returned to finish the album, his composition: "The D.W. Suite" was the result. The song is a wonderful tribute to the memory of Dennis.

I'm sure every Beach Boy fan can recall where and when they heard the tragic news of Denny's passing. In an interview with the Australian edition of Rolling Stone Magazine, July 1984, Christine McVie said that she was in Portugal when word reached her. "My secretary called me up at eight in the morning. I knew something was wrong. She said, "Dennis drowned today". And my first reaction was to say, "My God, is he all right?" I still really can't believe it. He just seemed indestructible."

Even though I had the opportunity to obtain new information from sources about Denny's last period of his life I chose not to, but the lingering question to me was, "Why his downward spiral"? There are many theories floating around out there like; his always being insecure and needing acceptance, his searching for an unfailing love, his need to love himself properly and finding unconditional love, how alcoholism and drug use

156

slowly took over as a disease he didn't realize as happening, etc.

I myself, believe that Denny has found what he was searching for and is experiencing it now. I also believe that he loved his family, his friends, and his fans and was unaware of what was happening to him. Even in his pain and misfortune towards the end, I think there was something about his life that can inspire us. It was his heart. Once on stage before singing, "You Are So Beautiful To Me", he said, "I know that not one of us is perfect, I know I'm not perfect, but the closest thing to being perfect is having us up here and you there going oooh"!

For Dennis

Eyes like stars sparkle and die
and cycle into new stars, new eyes.

The answer is outside our window.
Astronomers look
for the beginning
and find there is no end.

Down to earth,
there are frozen lines,
winter trees,
stalled cars in dirty snow,
sorrow over endings.

The real world is through the window,
infinite, ageless.
Though a clear veil
keeps us distant,
the soul of what
we can never prove
keeps us close.

—*Belinda Subraman*

On December 28th, 1983, Dennis Wilson died in an accidental drowning while diving in California harbor waters. He was 39 years old.

BBFUN Quarterly newsletter

VOL. IX, NO. 1   Published by The Beach Boys United (BBFUN), the Official Beach Boys Fan Club   **FEBRUARY 1984**

In Memoriam

DENNIS WILSON

Since his death, December 28, 1983, my thoughts have been a jumbled mess. However, I now have them in order and would like to share them with you. I don't want to go too far into detail but I would like to touch on Dennis' gererosity, zest for life and sensitivity.

My first thoughts fall upon Dennis' generosity. He had a bigger heart than anyone I've ever known. With no real attachment to material things, he seemed to be constantly giving things away. Sometimes he would give away his most personal possessions and many of us who were close to him thought he might be too generous. Dennis was continually trying to be the Good Samaritan, offering to help sometimes whether it was necessary or not.

Dennis was a very vital and alive person. He had a flair for living life to its fullest.

What seemed to be an endless amount of energy drove him to sample everything life had to offer. Because of this it was sometimes very hard to work for him, but little dampened his enthusiasm for just being alive.

One of my most tender memories of Dennis was when I asked him to be godfather to my daughter Bria. He was so touched by this that he cried. Afterwards many times he was with her he tried to teach her the Lord's Prayer. Many of his dealings in his professional as well as his private life have been clouded by his outlandish behavior but no one can dispute his concern for children. For example: his favorite charity was the Special Olympics and at his funeral friends were asked to make donations in his name instead of sending flowers. I believe that because Dennis was such a big kid himself he could focus on a child's need easier than the rest of us sometimes can.

My memories of Dennis are very complex, and it's very important to me that the good things Dennis has done outshine the shaded incidents that the media most like to focus on in someone like Dennis' passing. In closing I would just like to say I don't think of Dennis as being gone as his spirit will live on in our hearts forever. No-one can take away the beautiful memories that we have, like how special he could make you feel or his showing up barefoot with that special smile that only he had.

CHRIS KABLE

Farewell my friend
My beautiful friend
Farewell
You take the high road
I'll take the low road
And we'll meet again
Farewell my friend

I love you
In a funny way
You take the high road
I'll take the low road
And we'll meet again
Farewell my friend
I want to see you again

Oh farewell
Farewell
Oh I want to see you again
Farewell
Oh I'm on the mountain again
Oh farewell

THE
BEACH BOYS
(YESTERDAY)

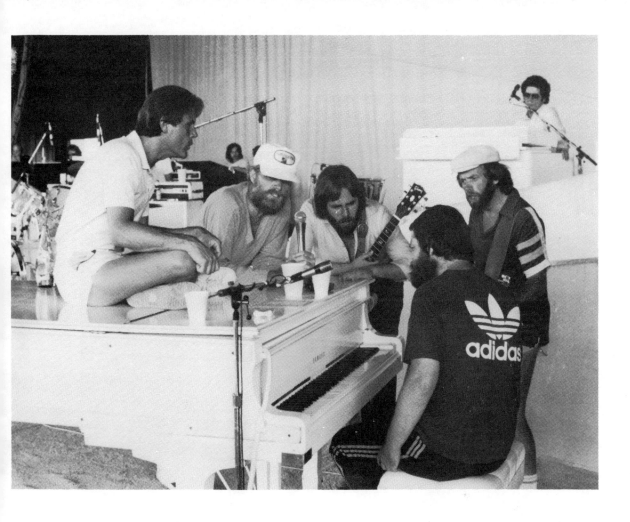

Rehearsal, Summer 1979 - Pine Knob, MI.

Carl Wilson

Al Jardine

Dennis Wilson

Mike Love

Bruce Johnston

Brian Wilson

Afterword

The Beach Boys, after Denny's death, have continued to be one of the top touring bands today. While they came through Tulsa for a May 12th, 1990 concert a fellow photographer, Donna Driesel, and myself were able to get some photos. Here are some of the shots. Mike Love wasn't there that day.

Best Wishes to The Beach Boys and may they continue to give us more of their great music.

173

AFTERWORD 1999

Well, it's just one year until the big 2000 and a lot has changed since this book first came out in 1991. Carl and Audree Wilson are gone,as well as Dennis, Brian has continued to go through many changes with his life and those around him and the future of The Beach Boys is still up in the air.

I met with The Beach Boys and Audree just before a concert in Tulsa right after my book came out. Audree told me how much she loved the book, which meant a great deal to me. Bruce Johnston told me stories behind some of the photos that are in the book. Mike Love said some comments that only he could, and I won't repeat them here. Al was cool, Carl was emotional. I realized Carl's very sensitive nature, which probably contributed to his artistic and musical talent.

Who can now replace Carl? The answer has to be no one. I've heard many stories about the kindness of Carl and it goes along with stories of Dennis, of course Dennis had that very wild streak in him unlike Carl. It seems like there are many nice traits running in the Wilson clan.

Who could ever replace Carl's voice? Of course, the answer again is no one. Whenever I hear Carl's version of "I Can Hear Music" I get chills up my spine. His work with The Beach Boys has left a legacy of beautiful music. From the early teenage songs right up to their more mature work it is a library of music with something for everyone.

I'm amazed at The Beach Boys music when I listen to it, not just the volume of the work, but also the beauty of it, the harmonies, the emotion, the feelings it brings to my soul. Music is truly a wonderful gift and Brian, Dennis, Carl, Al, Mike and all the other musicians who have contributed to The Beach Boys music have left a precious gift for us all.

When we are feeling down, there are songs to lift up our spirits. When we are in a meditative frame of mind we can put on "Pet Sounds", or a host of other music. When we want to celebrate, or be happy there is a large selection we can pick from. They say that music is the language of the soul so I think we can say that The Beach Boys are America's poets.

Appendix

A portion of the proceeds from this book is going to a California drug and alcohol rehabilitation center in Dennis Wilson's name.

Some other good programs that the reader may wish to get involved in are:

* **The Make A Difference Foundation**
  P. O. Box 1011
  Raleigh, NC (27602) USA

This is a non-profit organization dedicated to combating drug and alcohol abuse among youth via a pro-responsibility message.

* **The Special Olympics, Inc.**
  1350 New York Ave. N.W. • Suite 500
  Washington, D.C. (20005) USA

This is a non-profit organization helping disabled children and young adults through athletic events and other services. The Special Olympics was one of Denny's favorite charities.

List of Beach Boys (and related) Clubs Worldwide

1- Beach Boys Britian
   attn: Val Johnson
   3, Mill Grove
   Lutterworth
   Leicestershire
   LE17 4BS   England
   E-Mail:
v.johnson-howe@bssgroup.com
                    index.html

2- Break Away with
   Brian Wilson
   2049 Century Park East
   Suite 2450
   Los Angeles, CA 90067
   www.celebritymerch.com
   and; http:members.aol.
   com/_ht_a/Wilsonclb/

3- Beach Boys Fan Club
   (this is the official club)
   Mail Stop 504
   252 Convention Center Dr.
   Las Vegas, NV 89109

   www.mindspring.com/
   ~sfrazier/bbfc.htm

4- Mike Love Fan Club
   attn: Pat Ferrelli
   114 Gov. Winthrop Rd.
   Somerville, MA 02145

   www.mikelovefanclub.com

5- Endless Summer Quarterly
   P.O. Box 470315
   Charlotte, NC   28247

   esqeditor@aol.com

6- California Saga
   (German BB's Fan Club)
   attn: Heinz Drozella
   Eichberg str.48 D 79,
   Friedburg, Germany

7- Mike Kowalski Fan Club
   attn: Chris Dolbeare
   465 Tremont Street
   Berry, IL   62312

8- Friends of Dennis
   Wilson
   attn: Chris Duffy
   1381 Marie Way
   San Jose, CA 95117

List of Beach Boys Clubs (continued)

9- Beach Boys Stomp
   22 Avondale Road
   Wealdstone
   Middlesex
   HA3 7RE   England

10- Beach Boys Japan
    Shuhei Tsuchikawa
    Room 501, Tashiro-En
    93, Shinikecho 4 chome,
    Chikusa-ku, Nagoya
    464   Japan

11- Surfers Rule
    Goran Tannfelt
    Grev Turegatan 71
    114 38   Stockholm
              Sweden

12- Beach Boys/
    Brian Wilson Espana
    c/ Esgueva No. 15,1~A
    47.003   Valladolid
                      Spain

13- Beach Boys Australia
    P.O. Box 106
    North Strathfield
    2137   Australia

Photo Credits (By Page Numbers)

Abbreviations: **TL** = Top Left   **TR** = Top Right
                      ML = Middle Left   **MR** = Middle Right
                      BL = Bottom Left   **BR** = Bottom Right

Photo opposite the D.W. Suite:
          Detail of Beach Boys PR photo, collection of Brian Berry

Page 22:   Newspaper Ad For PACIFIC OCEAN BLUE, collection of Gayle Kettler

Page 23:   Photo, by George Fowler, collection of Steve Mayo

Page 24:   Same as page 23.

Page 25:   Collection of Hal Blaine

Pages 26-29:   All photos collection of Brian Berry

Page 30:   TL, BR - collection of Brian Berry / BL, TR collection of Priscilla Smits

Page 31:   All photos, collection of Brian Berry

Page 33:   Photo, collection of Hal Blaine / color design, Ed Wincentsen

Page 36:   TL - photo, by Paul Rambo / collection of Gayle Kettler
               TR - photo, by Nancy-Barr Brandon / collection of Linda Eiden
               ML, BR, BL - collection of Priscilla Smits
               MR - collection of Brian Berry

Page 40:   Top - collection of Priscilla Smits
               Middle, Bottom - Photos by Brian Berry

Page 41:   TL - collection of Brian Berry / Other photos by Brian Berry

Page 42:   Bottom, collection of Brian Berry

Page 43:   All photos, collection of Brian Berry

Page 44:   Top, BL - by Brian Berry
               BR - by Arlene Richie / Media Sources

Page 45:   TL - collection of Chris Duffy
               TR - collection of Priscilla Smits
               BL - collection of Annette Alwan
               BR - photo, by Brian Berry

Page 47:	Photo, collection of Brian Berry / color design, Ed Wincentsen
Page 50:	Top photo, by Brian Berry Middle photo, by Fred Vail Bottom photo, by Steve Mayo
Pages 52, 53:	All photos, by Steve Mayo
Page 54:	Collection of Brian Berry
Page 57:	Photo, by Brian Berry / color design, Ed Wincentsen
Page 60:	Collection of Brian Berry
Page 61:	Photo, by Rick Colville
Page 62:	Photo, by Brian Berry
Page 64:	Photo, by Brian Berry
Page 66:	Photo, by Annie Leibovitz / collection of Brian Berry
Page 67:	Collection of Brian Berry
Pages 68, 69:	All photos, by Nancy-Barr Brandon / collection of Linda Eiden
Page 71:	Photo, by Nancy-Barr Brandon / collection of Linda Eiden color design, Ed Wincensen
Page 73:	All photos, by Fred Vail
Page 74:	Photos by, Brian Berry
Page 75:	Top L/R - photos, by Brian Berry Other photos, by Arlene Richie / Media Sources
Pages 76-79:	All photos, by Brian Berry
Page 81:	Color photo, by Brian Berry
Page 83:	Collection of Brian Berry
Page 84:	Photo, by Ed Roach, © 1980, 1990
Pages 85, 86:	All photos, by Brian Berry
Page 87:	All photos, by Steve Mayo

Pages 88:   Photo, by Gary Nichamin / collection of Brian Berry

Page 89:   Photo, by Brian Berry / design, Ed Wincentsen

Page 90:   Collection of Brian Berry

Page 91:   Photo courtesy of The Beach Boys and Capitol Records
                 Collection of Domenic Priore

Page 93:   Collection of Domenic Priore

Page 96:   Collection of Domenic Priore

Page 99:   Detail of photo, by Brian Berry / color design, Ed Wincentsen

Page 101:   Photo, by Ed Roach © 1978, 1990

Pages 102,103: All photos, by Brian Berry

Page 104:   Collection of Brian Berry

Page 105:   Photo, by Brian Berry

Page 106,
    108-111:   All photos courtesy of the Estate of Dennis Wilson
                 (Page 109, photo by Ed Roach)

Page 113:   Photo, collection of Priscilla Smits / color design, Ed Wincentsen

Page 115:   Photo, by Tom Munson / collection of Gregg Lee

Page 116:   Both photos, collection of Betty Collignon

Page 122:   Concert poster, courtesy of Fred Vail

Page 123:   Photo, by Sandra Yates / collection of Fred Vail

Page 125:   Photo, by Ed Roach © 1979, 1990

Page 127:   Detail of photo, by Stuart Resor / color design, Ed Wincentsen

Pages 128, 129: Collection of Stuart Resor

Pages 130-132: All photos, by Stuart Resor

Pages 134, 135: Photo, by Stuart Resor

Other Titles available from Wynn Publishing.

 W y n n P u b l i s h i n g

Stevie Nicks, Rock's Mystical Lady
by Edward Wincentsen

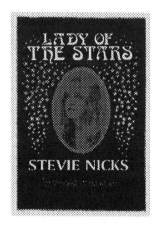

Lady of the Stars, Stevie Nicks
by Edward Wincentsen

Images of Jim Morrison
by Edward Wincentsen

COMING SOON !!!!!!!!!
BeatleToons, the story behind the cartoon Beatles.
By Mitchel Axelrod.   ISBN 0-9642808-7-6

Fleetwood Mac, Through the Years
By Edward Wincentsen. ISBN 0-9642808-6-8

These Books are Available at Wynnco.com
and other fine Bookstores

188

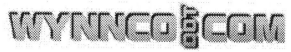

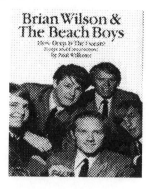